S0-EGQ-613

Incredible Hawaii

$4.50

Incredible
HAWAII

text by Terence Barrow
illustrations by Ray Lanterman

CHARLES E. TUTTLE COMPANY
Rutland · Vermont : Tokyo · Japan

Representatives

For Continental Europe:
BOXERBOOKS, INC., *Zurich*

For the British Isles:
PRENTICE-HALL INTERNATIONAL, INC., *London*

For Australasia:
BOOK WISE (AUSTRALIA) PTY. LTD.
104-108 Sussex Street, Sydney 2000

Published by the Charles E. Tuttle Company, Inc.
of Rutland, Vermont & Tokyo, Japan
with editorial offices at
Suido 1-chome, 2-6, Bunkyo-ku, Tokyo

© 1974 by Charles E. Tuttle Co., Inc.
All rights reserved

Library of Congress Catalog Card No. 74-77226
International Standard Book No. 0-8048 1137-7

First printing, 1974

Ninth printing, 1986

Printed in Japan

Table of Contents

 Publisher's foreword

THE INCREDIBLE IS A PART OF AMERICAN HISTORY AND
tradition—and our 50th State is certainly no exception.
This unique little book, incredible in its own way,
brings together the talents, knowledge and experience
of two well-known Hawaiian residents, artist-illustrator
Ray Lanterman and author-anthropologist Terence
Barrow.

Whatever their subject, the authors sail along with
justifiable confidence, opening to the reader, page
after page, vistas of a little-known Hawaii. At times
light-hearted, at other times serious, it is always a
readable and lookable book.

The authors delight in the unusual fact, whether it
be Oahu's marvelous and unusual water system,
song-making monarchs, or skiing on real snow on the
slopes of Mt. Mauna Kea, the highest point in the
Pacific area, reaching 13,796 feet above sea level—and
this is the essence of their book.

Tourists and residents alike will find *Incredible
Hawaii* a source of much pleasure which will lead
them to a greater awareness of these utterly fascinating
islands.

Acknowledgments

THE AUTHORS, BOTH WRITER AND ARTIST, WISH TO *acknowledge the help they have received in the making of this book. Mr. Charles E. Tuttle conceived the idea of* Incredible Hawaii, *then arranged for the book to become a reality.*

The authors wish to thank Mrs. R. A. Apple (better known to readers in Hawaii as Peg Apple) for reading the manuscript and for making suggestions for changes; and Mrs. K. A. Jordan, also of Honolulu, for typing the manuscript in a creative way. Mr. Robert E. Van Dyke, Hawaiiana collector and historian, lent valuable documents and gave of his wide experience. Mr. Joseph Feher of the Honolulu Academy of Arts kindly checked the illustrations. Thanks are also due for permission to quote from the popular song "My Little Grass Shack in Kealakekua Hawaii" (Copyright 1933, Miller Music Corporation: copyright renewed 1961, Miller Music Corporation). For the finished book, whatever its shortcomings, the authors assume full responsibility. Their aim is to provide an accurate yet light-hearted glimpse of some unusual and little known aspects of incredible Hawaii, hoping that the traveller will be entertained and the reader made more aware of these remarkable islands.

11

1 A Hawaiian story of creation

AN ANCIENT HAWAIIAN CREATION CHANT CALLED THE "Kumulipo" tells of the emergence of life out of cosmic darkness. In poetic terms it relates a story of evolution resembling the general concept of modern biology which is far from the Calvinist missionary doctrines that replaced it, namely that Adam and Eve and the world were created in a flash about five thousand years ago. Traditional Hawaiian thinking was more advanced on the subject.

The Hawaiians believed in Po, the fecund cosmic night in which was created the primitive forms of life such as coral animals, sea-urchins, barnacles and mollusca in general. The higher animals such as fish, reptiles and birds followed. Man and the gods emerged with Ao, the cosmic day which spread light, both physical and mental, over the world.

The primal parents of man, gods and islands were Papa, the Earth Mother, and Wakea, the Sky Father. Like the gods of Greek mythology, Papa and Wakea had their domestic troubles, mainly because Wakea took other wives. However, the Earth Mother also had a lover.

Interpreted symbolically, the "Kumulipo" offers a poetic story of creation in advance of European acceptance of the idea of evolution in the natural world, and it taught the relatively late advent of mankind.

2 Hawaiian origins and navigational skills

WHO ARE THE HAWAIIANS AND WHERE DID THEY COME from? How did they find these islands? When did they find them? These questions Hawaiian scholars have asked themselves with varying answers. Captain Cook puzzled over them when he found the Hawaiians speaking the same tongue as the Polynesians below the equator.

The endeavors of archaeologists, particularly of the Bishop Museum, give us a picture of settlement, not yet complete, that affords a view of the main events. The comparative study of artifacts such as adzes and fishhooks in relation to Polynesian voyaging and other features of the culture suggest the first of Hawaii's settlers came from the Marquesan Islands about the 7th century, followed by dominant, militaristic immigrants from the Society Islands about 500 years before Captain Cook's introduction of Western culture in 1778–79.

Polynesian navigators had no instruments to determine longitude and latitude but they knew which stars stood over each island. Wind patterns, ocean currents, bird flight, cloud formations and, above all, stars guided their paths. Large sea-going canoes made voyages of settlement bearing men, women, children, hogs, dogs, chickens, tools, seeds, roots and cuttings.

The Hawaiians are of this sailor stock of courageous men and woman who settled Polynesia.

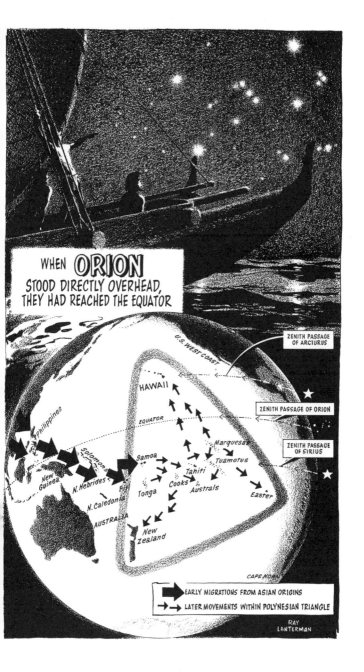

WHEN **ORION** STOOD DIRECTLY OVERHEAD, THEY HAD REACHED THE EQUATOR

ZENITH PASSAGE OF ARCTURUS

ZENITH PASSAGE OF ORION

ZENITH PASSAGE OF SIRIUS

U.S. WEST COAST

HAWAII

EQUATOR

Philippines

New Guinea

Solomons

N. Hebrides

N.Caledonia

Fiji

Tonga

Samoa

Cooks

Tahiti

Australs

Marquesa

Tuamotus

Easter

AUSTRALIA

New Zealand

CAPE HORN

EARLY MIGRATIONS FROM ASIAN ORIGINS

LATER MOVEMENTS WITHIN POLYNESIAN TRIANGLE

RAY LANTERMAN

3 The Hawaiian canoe

MAKING CANOES WAS AN OUTSTANDING POLYNESIAN
skill. Large ocean-going canoes carried the first
immigrants to Hawaii from the Marquesan and
Society Islands. Once settled, the Hawaiians developed
canoes suitable for inter-island travel, war and off-
shore fishing.

Canoes (*wa'a*), were vital to daily life. In 1778 there
were thousands in use in Hawaii. Over 3,000 came to
greet Captain Cook's ships when they anchored in
Kealakekua Bay.

Island travel was for trade, political or social
purposes. Channels were rough. Only seaworthy canoes
were safe when trade winds pressed against contrary
currents. Some canoes were sailed with tailored sheets
of pandanus matting. Others were paddled or both
paddled and sailed. The smallest fishing canoes could
be handled by one or two men; the largest war vessels
could carry a hundred or more people. Many war
canoes in the conquering navy of Kamehameha I
were large enough to mount light European cannon
of several kinds.

Canoe makers knew how to use their stone adzes
and secure the aid of the gods. At every stage from
felling the tree to finished vessel any mistake in ritual
endangered the mana or "good luck" of the canoe
and the life of the maker himself.

16

COMMUNITIES AFLOAT

CENTURIES BEFORE COLUMBUS OR MAGELLAN, POLYNESIANS WERE SAILING HUGE DOUBLE CANOES OVER THE VAST PACIFIC OCEAN, CARRYING PEOPLE, ANIMALS, PLANTS AND CULTURE TO THE FARTHEST ISLANDS

ROY LANTERMAN

4 The demi-god
who fished up islands

MAUI, THE SUPERMAN WHO FISHED UP ISLANDS AND performed many remarkable tasks, is known to Pacific islanders of Polynesia, Melanesia and Micronesia. Maui is one of the most lovable of all characters in Polynesian mythology because of his genial, mischievous nature. Often called "Maui-of-a-thousand-tricks," he well deserves this nickname.

Some stories say that Maui was still-born of a human mother, then cast into the sea, from which he emerged alive. He certainly was a supernatural child with godlike powers. In Hawaiian mythology he appears in relation to a specific place, such as Waianae on Oahu, at a cave above Hilo on the Wailuku River, and at Kahakuloa and Kauiki on the island of Maui.

He is said to have secured fire for mankind and lengthened the daylight hours by snaring the sun, which pleaded for life with the promise it would go slower across the sky in the future. Maui is also credited with pushing up the sky, but his most notable habit was that of fishing up islands from the sea bottom. The place where his sacred fishhook caught is known on some Pacific islands.

The 19th-century recorders of Hawaiian myths seem to have regarded the Maui stories as too childish to write down, so many of the tales of superman Maui are lost forever.

18

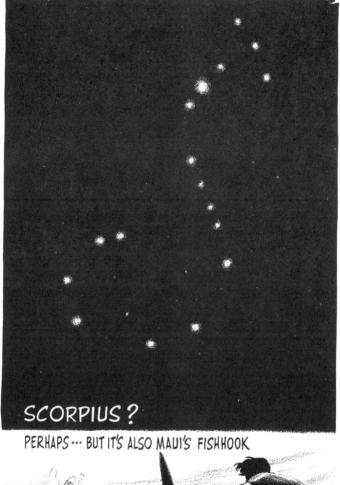

SCORPIUS?

PERHAPS ··· BUT IT'S ALSO MAUI'S FISHHOOK

5 Drifting islands of Hawaii

THERE HAVE BEEN MANY THEORIES TO EXPLAIN THE
origin of the Hawaiian chain of islands. Before modern
geophysical studies of the floor of the world's oceans,
a theory prevailed that the surface of the earth was a
more or less immovable crust. The Hawaiian Islands
were believed by some to be formed by outwelling
lava as a great rift or crack opened on the sea bottom.
It now appears more likely that tectonic plates of
earth's crust drift around the globe at a rate of about
seven feet per century.

According to the latter theory the vast Pacific plate
on which Hawaii sits glides over the earth's semi-fluid
under-crust like a gigantic raft, and as this plate passes
over a "hot spot" lava vent, islands are formed. The
Big Island of Hawaii is now passing over this great
vent and is thus still in formation. Some day Hawaii,
like the other islands, will have moved on, and a new
island will start to form. Islands appear to glide off
in a northwest direction, riding on a giant plate which
at its upper end moves under Japan and Asia, causing
earthquakes from time to time.

The Hawaiian Islands have been in the process of
creation and dissolution for about 20 million years.
The earliest undersea volcanic mountains to break sea
surface now stretch about 2,000 miles to the northwest
of the Big Island, some worn down to rocky pinnacles
or eroded to water-level reefs.

20

ISLANDS ON THE MOVE...?!

SCIENTISTS TELL US THAT THE HAWAIIAN ISLANDS ARE MOVING VERY SLOWLY TO THE NORTHWEST—

IF ALL THE WATER WERE DRAINED FROM THE PACIFIC, THE ISLANDS MIGHT LOOK SOMETHING LIKE THIS: RISING FROM THE OCEAN FLOOR

NIIHAU   KAUAI

OAHU

MOLOKAI

LANAI

KAHOOLAWE

MAUI

HAWAII

RAY LANTERMAN

VERTICAL SCALE GREATLY EXAGGERATED

6 The little people of the night

THE FIRST INHABITANTS OF THE HAWAIIAN ISLANDS ARE the *Keiki-o-ka'aina* (Children of the Land), little night creatures better known to Hawaii residents as Menehune.

They arc said to have lived in Hawaii before the Hawaiian ancestors arrived, and are still about. Reports of them are made from time to time today. The Menehune are described as a squat and rather ugly pigmy race with many of the traits of European elves, pixies, fairies, gnomes and trolls. They are known in all Polynesian islands. The Manahune of the Society and Cook Islands are of the same little race. The island of Kauai is said to be their original Hawaiian home.

Menehune are said to dislike being seen by mortals, yet some make human friends and generally children seem inoffensive to them. They do mankind favours if well treated, making in past times stone temples, fishponds and watercourses. In fact, they seem to enjoy working. They are gregarious, noisy, talkative little fellows, often up to some mischief; yet they prefer to live in lonely valleys, in the mountains, in caves, hollow logs or primitive huts.

The Menehune are believed to be supernatural creatures who have a distinct dislike of daylight. Where they came from and how many still live is quite unknown.

THE LITTLEST FOLKS
DID THE BIGGEST JOBS

7 Animal guardians of Hawaii

SUPERNATURAL SPIRITS AND GODS WERE AS REAL TO
the old Hawaiians as the actual world. Nothing of
importance was done without consulting occult, unseen
beings. Some of these are *aumakua*, a class of ancestral
guardians who inhabit the bodies of certain animals.

The three most favored *aumakua* were the shark,
lizard and owl. The family that adopted one particular
creature as its *aumakua* would not eat or harm it as it
was considered a protective guardian. The shark was
a fearful guardian to whom the dead were sometimes
fed to appease its spirit. Once a woman was grasped
at the ankle by a shark that was her family guardian.
She cried out its name and it let her go with an
apology for its mistake. Shark guardians aided their
patron family by driving fish into nets and warding
off evil.

Lizards in the form of geckoes were also very
effective guardians. Animal guardians were friendly
to the family that adopted them and unfriendly to
family enemies.

The flight of the owl or *pueo* was watched for an
omen of good or evil. To this day some Hawaiians
remember their family guardian and treat it with
respect.

24

FAMILY GUARDIANS

MANO THE SHARK

MO'O THE LIZARD

PUEO THE OWL

8 Dogs that did not bark

LONG AGO THE DOG AND THE PIG WERE BROUGHT FROM tropical Polynesia as food, and the rat came as an undesirable stowaway. The only land mammal at that time in Hawaii was a native bat, too small to eat. It is said the Hawaiian dog did not bark. Named *'ilio,* it lived on a diet of fish, coconut, scraps and poi—hence the name "poi dog" now given to any dog of doubtful ancestry. This old dog is pictured in rock art as a long, low-slung animal with a back-curling tail. When the *haole* or foreign dog was introduced, the Hawaiian dog became extinct as a separate species because of inbreeding and changed food habits.

The Hawaiian dog probably made whining or singing sounds like the "barkless" dogs of New Guinea to be seen in the Honolulu Zoo. At tabu times their snouts were tied to silence them. They were food, rarely companions, while their flesh was preferred to pork. The Reverend William Ellis in Hawaii in the 1820's saw 200 dogs baked for a single feast. Skin, hair, bone and teeth had other uses. Bone made excellent fishhooks and teeth were used in dancers' anklets. Even the *kahuna* could be paid in dogs for black magic, medicine or canoe building.

Spirit dogs are known in Hawaii. It is said they haunt Nu'uanu Valley; their figures are cut in the rocks near the Royal Mausoleum.

ILIO
THE QUIET CANINE

NO BOW-WOW HE!

THE POLYNESIAN DOG
BROUGHT BY THE EARLIEST HAWAIIANS
RARELY – IF EVER – –
DID ANY BARKING

RAY
LANTERMAN

9

The humuhumunukunukuapua'a and other fish

THERE IS A POPULAR SONG DATING BACK TO THE HAPPY pre–World War II days of Hawaii which uses a Hawaiian word that few visitors can pronounce or remember. The song goes: "I want to go back to my little grass shack in Ke-ala-ke-kua Hawaii where the *humuhumunukunukuapua'a* go swimming by. . ."

Simply speaking, *humuhumunukunukuapua'a* is a small fish made famous by its name, which literally means the fish of a family of fishes called "*humuhumu*" which has a snout like a pig. The *humuhumunukunukuapua'a* is no more than a very humble member of Hawaii's numerous species of inshore fish.

The fish fauna of the Hawaiian Islands derived largely from the tropical Philippine and Indonesian waters. They were carried on warm currents to the coasts of Hawaii over millions of years. New species of fish continue to arrive, some coming along as followers of slow-moving barges whose bottoms are trailing seaweed, as stray travellers on currents or by human introduction.

The fish population of Hawaii, so vital to the sustenance of the ancient Hawaiians, has suffered much from modern urbanization, particularly around Oahu. Artificial reefs of old automobiles are restoring fish life by providing shelter from predators, but the fight against over-fishing and pollution must go on if the fish are to return to their former abundance.

LAWAI'A ∞ FISHING

HUMUHUMUNUKUNUKUAPUA'A

KIHIKIHI

AHI TUNA

MALOLO FLYING FISH

HE'E OCTOPUS

A'U MARLIN

MAHIMAHI DOLPHIN

RAY LANTERMAN

10 The king of beasts in old Hawaii

THE POLYNESIAN SETTLERS OF HAWAII BROUGHT ONLY three edible mammals with them, the pig (*pua'a*), the dog (*'ilio*) and the rat (*'iole*). The seal and native bat were mammals which had reached the Hawaiian Islands before them. Man, regarded as an edible animal in the Polynesian Islands of New Zealand, the Marquesas group and Fiji, was not to our knowledge an item of diet in Hawaii. Had the Hawaiians lacked pigs, as did the Maori, cannibalism might have become part of old Hawaiian life.

The pig was a kind of "king of beasts" in Hawaii, much used in sacrifice to the gods by priests or as a means of identifying evil sorcerers by its movements, and as a table delicacy for men only. Contrary to most of mankind, the Hawaiians regarded the pig as an intelligent animal. Pigs, they said, were capable of recognizing a high chief living in exile by their manner of obediently raising their snouts to any anonymous noble.

As many as two thousand pigs were baked at great feasts. They were the prime item in trading with European ships. Boars' tusks were converted into very charming bracelets.

PUA'A
IMPORTANT PORKER

PIGS ARRIVED WITH THE EARLIEST POLYNESIAN COLONISTS AND HAVE ALWAYS BEEN AN INTEGRAL PART OF HAWAIIAN LIFE, ANCIENT AND MODERN

...A CEREMONIAL ANIMAL IN TIMES PAST...
...A VALUABLE FOOD SOURCE IN ANY TIME...
...AND OFTEN A FAMILY PET.

KAMAPUA'A, THE PIG GOD, TRIED TO CHARM PELE BY DISGUISING HIMSELF AS A HANDSOME FELLOW

NOTHING QUITE COMPARES WITH ROAST PIG DIRECT FROM THE *IMU* — UNDERGROUND STONE OVEN

RAY LANTERMAN

11 Banana, breadfruit and pandanus

THESE THREE TREES, BANANA, BREADFRUIT AND
pandanus, can be seen in abundance throughout the
Hawaiian chain. They rank next to the coconut tree
in usefulness.

Viable banana shoots came with the Polynesian
settlers to Hawaii. Many varieties were known to
them, and they were used for food or as offerings to
the gods. The leaves served as platters or wrappings,
and the trunks provided a silky thread or material
for a kind of bark-cloth.

The breadfruit, *Artocarpus altilis,* called *ulu,* was
also introduced from the South Pacific. It became
widely known after the H.M.S. *Bounty* went to Tahiti
to fetch young trees as a food source for Caribbean
slaves on a voyage which ended in mutiny. The fruit,
which can weigh up to ten pounds, resembles bread
when roasted or baked. The wood was used in many
ways while the milky sap sealed seams in canoe hulls.

The pandanus, better known by its Hawaiian name
hala, or *lau-hala* (after the leaf), has the common name
"screw pine" and the botanic name *Pandanus odoratis-
simus.* This tree has spreading aerial roots which give
it the fanciful name of "walking tree" as it appears to
be going somewhere. The pineapple-like fruits cause
some to think the tree is the source of pineapples. The
fruit is partly edible and was used after careful prepa-
ration, but the chief use of *hala* to the Hawaiians was
the leaves which were made into matting, sandals,
fans, baskets, pillows and canoe sails.

THE
WALKING
TREE
...AND OTHERS

BREADFRUIT

BANANAS GROW
ALMOST ANYWHERE
IN THE ISLANDS

ROASTING BREADFRUIT
ON AN OPEN *IMU*

RAY
LANTERMAN

12 Poi: the Hawaiian staff of life

IF THE COCONUT WAS THE PACIFIC ISLANDERS' FRUIT
of heaven, taro root was their staff of life. Poi made
from taro was the single most important food of the
Hawaiians. Poi is mashed vegetable matter, usually
from taro root, but breadfruit and sweet potato were
also used.

Cooked in an earth oven called *imu*, the root or
fruit was scraped and beaten to a pasty consistency
with a stone pounder, then fermented according to
taste. Poi pounding was usually the work of men, yet
women were able to take over in necessity.

Water was added to the first pounding stage to form
the right consistency. Hand kneading followed, with
the addition of more water to make one-finger or two-
finger poi. What is commonly called "three-finger
poi" is more of a joke than a reality. Poi of gruel-like
consistency was not served to guests as it was considered
very impolite to serve thin poi.

Before taro poi could be made, the corm had to be
grown in either mountain valley plantations or lowland
fields. There were many varieties of taro, some grown
on dry land and others in swampy fields. Each kind
had its own taste and texture, and was a most
wonderful food, especially for the old and babies who
could not handle the "hard foods" of Hawaiian
cookery.

1·finger — STICKY-GOOEY

2·finger — GOOEY-DAMP

3·finger — RUNNY-WET

POI

THIS NUTRITIOUS MAINSTAY OF POLYNESIAN DIET COMES ANY WAY YOU LIKE IT

NOWADAYS, POI IS MADE BY MACHINE: THE EARLY HAWAIIANS MADE IT BY POUNDING THE COOKED TARO CORMS TO A THICK PASTA

TARO GROWING IN FLOODED PATCH

TARO CORM

SOME IRREVERENT PERSONS HAVE BEEN KNOWN TO SAY POI TASTES LIKE LIBRARY PASTE!

STONE POI POUNDER

RAY LANTERMAN

13 Cocus nucifera: the tree of life

THE COCONUT PALM, OR NIU, AS IT IS NAMED BY MOST Polynesians, was an important tree in old Hawaii. Its nuts provided food and drink while the trunk and leaves had many domestic uses. On some Pacific islands life was impossible without the coconut palm. The Hawaiians were not completely dependent on it, yet its products were used in many ways.

The nuts provided refreshing drink, oil came from the copra, husk fibre made cordage for tying, whole nuts were used as offerings to the gods; leaves were plaited into baskets, mats and platters, and also served in religious ceremonies. The dense trunk wood had many uses, such as for carved hula drum bases. Coconut-meat cream was mashed into cooked taro, sweet potato or breadfruit.

In Hawaii and most of Polynesia, the coconut palm is one of the most useful and romantic of trees. It symbolizes Hawaii better than the *kukui* or "candlenut tree" which is the State tree. In the Pacific it is truly the tree of life, or as some say, the Tree of Heaven.

The life of the coconut palm matches a man's natural span. One planted at birth can provide the needs of an individual for his lifetime.

The first coconut palms grown in Hawaii sprouted from nuts brought by Polynesian settlers. Hawaii is thought to be beyond the range of natural drift plantings, as the nut of the coconut will not remain viable in salt water beyond four months.

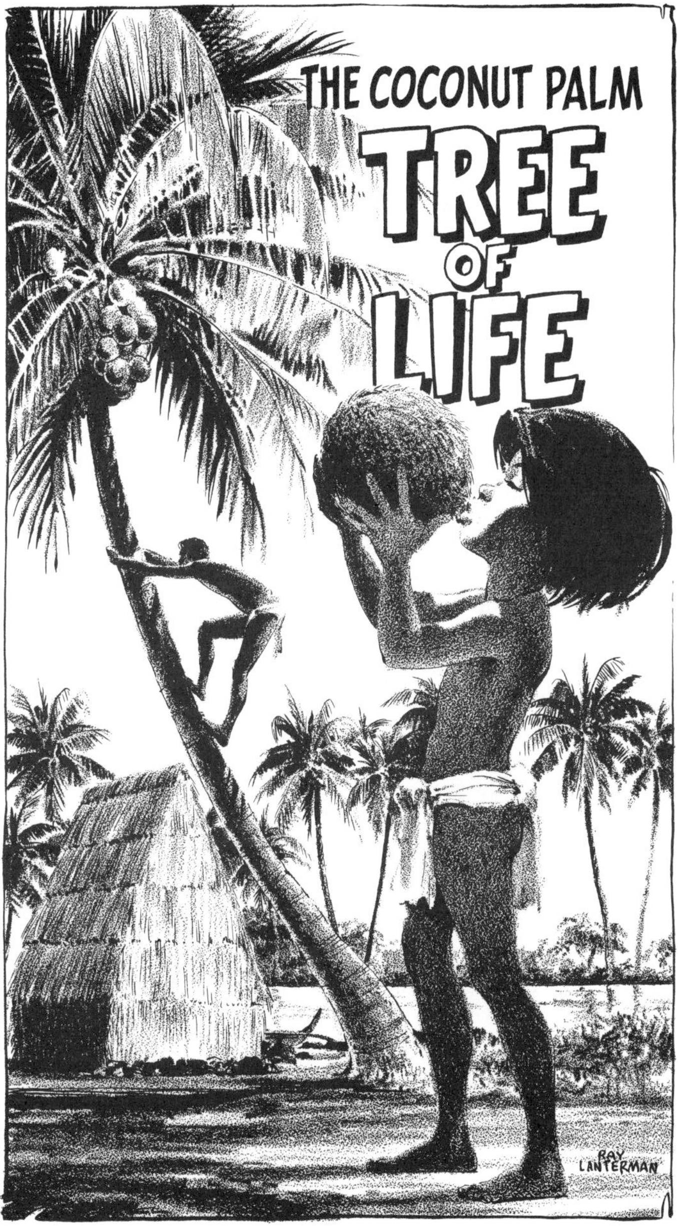
THE COCONUT PALM
TREE OF LIFE
RAY LANTERMAN

14 Tree oddities of Hawaii

THAT THE TROPICAL TREES OF GARDENS AND ROADWAYS are of foreign origin usually surprises visitors to Hawaii. Before foreign plants and trees were grown here and their cultivation made possible by piped water, Hawaii was barren in areas such as Nuʻuanu Valley, which today is rich with luxuriant greenery. Some of the tree imports have curious fruit.

The "dead rat tree" is a native of Central Africa where it is called *baobab*. Scientists know it by the name of *Adansonia digitata*. It has seed pods of a rattish form with fur-like skin of brown, which hang on cords like corpses of rats suspended by their tails.

The "cannon ball tree," which science calls *Couroupita guianensis*, is a native of tropical America. Racemes of pungent exotic flowers grow out from the woody trunk, and large globular fruits which sometimes attain the size of the human head hang down like iron cannon balls on long stringers.

The "sausage tree," *Kigelia pinnata*, is a native of tropical West Africa that has elongated fruits hanging down like so many sausages on cordlike stalks several feet in length.

In Honolulu these three trees may be seen at Foster Garden. In their native lands all three are valuable to mankind, furnishing food, dishes, fibres, leafy green vegetables, hard woods and water.

OF CANNON BALLS SAUSAGES AND DEAD RATS...

THE SAUSAGE TREE

RAY LANTERMAN

THE 'CANNON BALL' IS ABOUT THE SIZE OF A COCONUT

THE CANNON BALL TREE

"DEAD RAT"

15 Temples and shrines of Hawaii

PILES OF ROCKS WHICH ARE THE REMAINS OF TEMPLES called *heiau* are to be seen throughout the Hawaiian Islands. Religious life centered about these temples before the coming of Christianity. Old engravings and drawings show them as grand arrangements of wooden gods, oracle towers, houses and enclosures. The 1819 edict of Kamehameha II which abandoned the old gods caused a general destruction of the temples by fire. It is said that when a *heiau* on Oahu was put to the torch, the glow of its fires could be seen on Kauai. Stone foundations and a hundred or so wooden gods in museums are vestiges of a lost religion and a way of life that endured a thousand years.

Some of the former glory of the temples may be seen in the restoration of the *heiau* at Hale-o-Keawe at the City of Refuge at Honaunau Bay. Not all temples were grand. There were family *heiau* and small shrines set aside for particular uses. All high chiefs were priests but some were specialists in consecration rites. In acts of human sacrifice specialists were vital to correct ceremony.

White bark-cloth, sacred to the gods, adorned temples, houses, oracle towers or images, and it floated like banners in the breeze. The earliest drawing of a temple was made at Waimea on Kauai in 1778 by James Webber, the artist with Captain Cook.

THE HEIAU
...PLACE OF SACRIFICIAL FIRES... SACRED RITES...

HALE O KEAWE, HEIAU ON THE KONA COAST, WAS THE DEPOSITORY OF BONES OF ANCIENT KINGS. IT HAS BEEN RESTORED TO LOOK LIKE THIS 1823 VIEW

AFTER A DRAWING BY REV. WILLIAM ELLIS

RAY LANTERMAN

16 Waikiki and its kahuna stones

OVER THE CENTURIES THOSE WITH TIME TO RELAX have been attracted to Waikiki. A unique haven of beaches and sheltered waters with a rare climate of warmth, combined with cool northeast trade winds softened by the barrier of the Koʻolau range, creates Waikiki. After the islands had been conquered, King Kamehameha set up a palace of wood and stone there, and his descendants and the elite have favored it as a retreat ever since.

Today the scene has changed but much of the charm remains. The long stretches of beach from Ala Moana Park to Diamond Head can be walked with a few short bypasses such as at the Ala Wai Yacht Harbor. The concrete highrise boom of the last decade has not changed the sea front with its blue horizons. A century ago coconut groves, fish ponds and swampy rice fields occupied the land where today modern hotels jostle for space.

The "kahuna stones" in the beach park next to the SurfRider Hotel are a vestige of the ancient lore. They are said to possess healing powers transferred to them by four priests from Tahiti: Kapaemahu, Kahaloa, Kapuni and Kinohi, who lived in Hawaii before the reign of Oahu's ancient ruler, Kakuhihewa. Before returning to their homeland in the South Pacific, they endowed the stones with their power to heal, and the Hawaiians have held them in reverence ever since.

THE HEALING STONES AT KUHIO BEACH

YOU CAN SEE THEM TODAY,
UNDER THE HALA TREE ... RIGHT BY THE SIDEWALK

RAY
LANTERMAN

17 Black magic arts of the old kahuna

A CURIOUS FACT OF POLYNESIAN RELIGIOUS BELIEF WAS the widely held conviction that there was no such thing as a natural death.

In Hawaiian or other Polynesian eyes a person died from an obvious cause, such as a blow from a club, or from malicious magic. The curses of the practitioners of black magic, the dreaded *kahuna 'ana'ana*, were greatly feared, yet if such curses failed to reach their mark or were turned away by superior magic, their evil returned to harm the man who first issued them.

This fear of evil magic and black magicians caused chiefs to keep scrap bowls guarded over by special attendants whose duty it was to gather uneaten food, hair clippings and nail parings, so that such waste could be disposed of secretly. Those who wished to do evil to another individual had an enormous advantage if they acquired anything that had come into contact with the body of the intended victim, such as food scraps or bodily waste of any kind. Such substances could be burnt in small stone cups with suitable incantations, thus making a more effective magic than mere praying to death. Black magicians could be hired. Theirs was a dangerous occupation because any unsuccessful magic turned on the man who made it. Consequently those practitioners who stayed alive had a record of success.

Felled from afar

18 Desecration of the dead

HAWAIIAN TRADITIONAL CULTURE HAD CERTAIN
barbaric customs. Like other cultures of the world,
it had both its pleasant and unpleasant ways. Pre-
Christian Hawaii retained the Polynesian belief that
friends were those of blood kin or who had some tribal
connection. Others were suspect strangers or outright
enemies.

Before King Kamehameha unified the islands by
conquest they were divided into minor kingdoms that
were perennially at odds with one another. Open war
with quick death or victory was an accepted way of
life. Many chiefs and commoners ended their days as
sacrificial victims in temple compounds. But there
were deaths the Hawaiians feared more. One was
magic directed against them by priests, the dreaded
kahuna ʻanaʻana who could pray them to death. Also
feared were the thieves who might desecrate bones
by converting them into fish hooks or embedding teeth
in wooden spittoons as the ultimate humiliation both
to the dead and to living relatives. The spirit was
believed to possess in life or death a *mana*—prestige,
or spiritual essence, that could be harmed by magic.
Kamehameha was ensured against such desecration
by having his body secreted in a hidden cave.

Hatred and revenge thrived in old Hawaii. The
death of an enemy was a delight which could be
savored more particularly if his bones could be
desecrated.

46

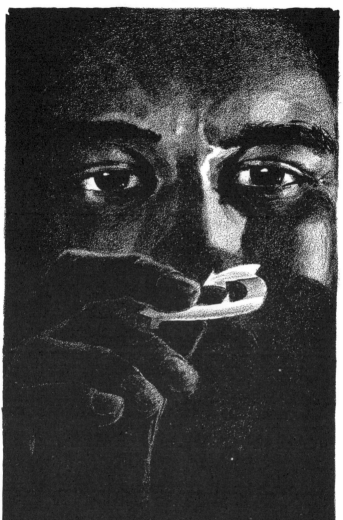

don't let him get at your bones

RAY
LANTERMAN

19 The tattooists' art in old Hawaii

HAWAIIAN TATTOOING CAME TO AN END SOON AFTER the tabu system was abolished in the 19th century. Drawings made by early visitors, written descriptions and the skin of mummified bodies found in burial caves are the sources of our knowledge of the art.

Men and women were tattooed at an early age by highly skilled, or less-skilled, craftsmen according to rank. The tattooists' cutting "combs" were made from bird wing bones dipped in a black pigment which turned blue under the skin. Fishbones were also used as implements. Aristocrats were tattooed to add to their beauty but slaves or *kauwa* were often marked with a spot on their foreheads, or lines which branded them as the property of a chief or a family.

Tattoo design motifs resemble bark-cloth patterns. A geometric, rectilinear style prevails, yet free miscellaneous designs were used. In post-European times objects such as the musket, letters, goats and horses made their appearance in tattoo. The striking feature of Hawaiian tattoo is its asymmetry: half a face or body might be tattooed while the other half was left plain.

Tattoo was also used as a mark of mourning on the death of a chief or after a calamity. When King Kamehameha I died some had his name tattooed on their arms. The tongue was also occasionally tattooed at time of mourning.

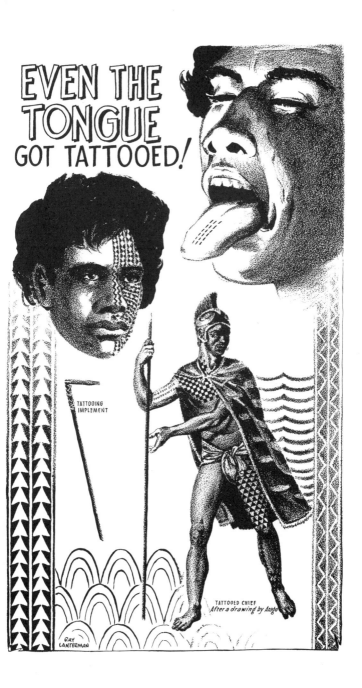

EVEN THE TONGUE GOT TATTOOED!

TATTOOING IMPLEMENT

TATTOOED CHIEF
After a drawing by Arago

RAY LANTERMAN

20 Games and leisure in old Hawaii

POLYNESIAN LIFE IN PREHISTORIC HAWAII WAS FAR FROM easy. The labor of working taro fields, fishing at sea, carrying water, tending pigs and dogs, making things without metal tools, meeting tax tributes and other demands put a strain on everyone for much of the year. Starvation threatened and even in good times hunger was common. Every act of life was surrounded by prohibitive tabus for high born and lowly alike, while the possibility of being sacrificed to the gods or dying in war was ever present.

Yet the happy-go-lucky Polynesians remained full of fun and took life's burdens lightly. In the middle of October the annual four-month *makahiki* festival was begun. Taxes payable to overlords were cleared and song and dance enlivened the scene. Tabus were relaxed and warfare abandoned while great tournaments of wrestling, foot-racing, boxing, spear-throwing and other sports held the attention of all. Surfing, diving, canoe racing, sledding, stilt walking, kite flying and bowling contests added excitement to the days.

The game of draughts or checkers, called *konane*, had wide popularity. Men gambled with abandon so it is little wonder this particular pastime was condemned by the missionaries. A more innocent play was cat's cradle, a game using looped string, which formed a great number of patterns to accompanying chants.

ALL WORK AND NO PLAY? *Hardly.*

FROM PRE-HISTORY TIMES TO NOW, HAWAII'S KIDS HAVE CONTRIVED INTRICATE CAT'S CRADLE DESIGNS

KONANE IS PLAYED WITH BLACK AND WHITE PEBBLES···ANCIENT BOARDS WERE OF STONE, WITH AN INDENTED SURFACE. TODAY'S KONANE KITS CONTAIN WOODEN BOARDS AND COMPLETE INSTRUCTIONS

NEVER USED IN HAWAII'S WARS, THE BOW AND ARROW WAS A CHILD'S TOY IN FORMER DAYS·· NOW, ARCHERY RANGES ARE FOUND IN PUBLIC PARKS ALONGSIDE GOLF DRIVING RANGES AND TENNIS COURTS

UNDER THE BANNER OF *LONO*, WRESTLING, BOXING AND FENCING MATCHES TOOK PLACE DURING THE ANNUAL MAKAHIKI

SMALL-FRY AMUSED THEMSELVES FOR HOURS TRYING TO CATCH THE BALL IN THE RING

RAY LANTERMAN

21 Surfing on land and sea

THERE WERE TWO KINDS OF "SURFING" IN OLD HAWAII, one on the sea and the other on land. Sea surfing is of two basic kinds; body surfing without a board, and surfing with a board. Formerly boards ranged in size from light boards to those weighing as much as 200 pounds and measuring 17 feet or more in length. Tradition required they be made with stone adzes from a tree at least as wide as the board, so the labor was great.

Sledding is a kind of surfing on land. The Hawaiians call it *holua*, an ancient sport of kings that is now extinct. Only the tracks remain. The sled consisted of two runners about 11 feet long set closely together with separating crossbars and covered with matting. Sled tracks up to 600 feet long were constructed from rocks on a suitable hillside and covered with slippery grass to provide a smooth running surface. It was a hazardous sport, and as the track was narrow only one sled could run at a time, so abreast racing was not feasible. The aim was distance, and the sled that ran farthest won.

The revival of *holua* would provide an exciting spectator sport.

SPEEDY AT SEA ••• FAST ON THE GRASS

THE MODERN SURFBOARD—
SMALLER AND MANY TIMES
LIGHTER THAN THOSE OF
ANCIENT HAWAII

RAY
LANTERMAN

22 Sacred hula of old Hawaii

TODAY'S HULA GIRL IN TI-LEAF SKIRT IS AS HAWAIIAN
as poi. Hula is usually entertainment, with lovely
hula hands and swaying hips telling a romantic story.
In ancient times hula was mainly a sacred art, danced
for the gods who aided mankind, but even then the
secular hula was danced.

Curious things happened to hula over the past 150
years. In 1819 the Hawaiians struck the first blow
when they destroyed their own temples. Then the
missionaries came and they thought the hula lewd.
King Kamehameha III attempted to revive hula
about 1840; however, it was not until the reign of
King David Kalakaua (1874 to 1891) that hula was
effectively revived as an art.

Hula is a Polynesian action dance with bodily
movements following the song or chant. The modern
instruments are old forms; the drum (*hula pahu*), split
bamboo sticks (*hula pu'ili*), gourd rattles with feather
ornaments (*hula 'uli'uli*), castanet pebbles (*hula 'ili'ili*)
and hardwood sticks (*hula kala'au*).

Men performed the sacred hulas in olden times.
Drawings made by the early explorers show them as
vigorous and manly exponents of the dance. Hula
teachers were sacred persons inspired by the gods. Pele,
the Fire Goddess, inspired her followers with hula
chants that are still remembered. The supreme
patroness of hula was Hi'iaka, to whom many cycles of
storytelling were dedicated. Laka was also invoked.

54

RELIGIOUS RITE
FESTIVAL DANCE
COURT ENTERTAINMENT
STORY-TELLER
PARTY STOPPER
THAT'S THE HAWAIIAN **HULA**

MALE DANCERS
FROM EARLY DRAWINGS
BY CHORIS & WEBBER.

IT MUST HAVE BEEN EASIER TO KEEP YOUR EYES ON THE HANDS IN THE OLD DAYS ... WHEN THE GENTS WERE OFTEN OUT FRONT...

RAY LANTERMAN

23 Cockfighting as a sport

GALLUS GALLUS IS A JUNGLE BIRD FROM SOUTHEAST
Asia, of handsome appearance with a proud strutting
manner and flaunting tail feathers. It is little wonder
that the Hawaiians, having such a bird, were devoted
to cockfighting.

Some birds were trained to fight, but the main value
of the hen and cock was food. Some cocks ended their
days as offerings to the gods, while the glossy tail
feathers were often used to ornament the capes of the
lesser chiefs.

Warriors of old Hawaii were likened to fighting
birds. The crested helmets and great capes of high
chiefs resemble bird crests and wings. Cockfighting
as a sport has been practiced in Hawaii by immigrants,
particularly the Filipino community. For centuries the
Philippine group has ranked cockfighting high as a
sport.

Wherever men have virile cock birds they set them
fighting. The Greeks, Romans, English and colonial
Americans were devoted to cockfights.

Cockfighting has been illegal in Hawaii for decades
yet there are signs that "bloodless" cockfighting may
be permitted or sanctioned some day.

56

24 Abolition of sex discrimination

A FRIGHTENING IDEA IN OLD HAWAII WAS THAT OF A man sitting down to eat with a woman. It was tabu by the laws separating men and women. Ceremonials in temples and the eating of pork and bananas were tabu to women; they were not permitted to approach men engaged in crafts such as canoe building.
It was "a man's world" in which women often held great power because of high birth, yet were barred from things even common men enjoyed.

All tabus came to an end after the advent of European ideas, iron tools, tailored clothes and the Christian religion. A year before the arrival of the missionaries in 1820 King Kamehameha II ordered his people to abandon the old gods, temples and images. In 1819 he had a feast prepared and ordered prohibited foods such as fowl served to his wives and the women with them, then he sat down to eat with them, directing others to do likewise. When shouts of horror from the crowd died down, several chiefs followed his example.

The instigator of tabu removal was the strong-minded Kaahumanu, widow and former favorite wife of King Kamehameha I. She became regent on the death of her husband and had much to gain from elimination of the laws of sexual segregation.

WOMEN'S LIB
HAWAIIAN STYLE

LIHOLIHO (KAMEHAMEHA II) CONFOUNDED EVERYBODY WHEN HE ACTUALLY SAT DOWN TO EAT *WITH WOMEN*! THEY ALL THOUGHT HE'D BE STRUCK DEAD ON THE SPOT FOR SUCH AN APPALLING BREACH OF TIME-HONORED SOCIAL TABUS.

RAY LANTERMAN

25 A challenge to the Fire Goddess Pele

KAPIOLANI, HIGH CHIEFESS AND WIFE OF NAIHE, A
chief of Ka'awaloa of the Big Island, stands high on
the list of Hawaii's heroic women. She openly
confronted Pele, the Fire Goddess who lives in Kilauea
volcano.

On the edict of Kamehameha II in 1819, the old
tabu (*kapu*) system had been overthrown by the
Hawaiians and the old gods went with it. Supporters
of the old religion took up arms to support their faith,
but Christianity had come to stay and they were
defeated.

Kapiolani was an ardent convert to Christianity, and
she decided to give visible evidence of her faith by
confronting Pele and breaking once and for all the
awe her people felt for that capricious goddess. She
made her way to Kilauea, descended several hundred
feet into the fire pit, ate the *ohelo* berries sacred to
Pele and cast stones into the flames below. Then she
proclaimed "Jehovah is my God—it is my God and
not Pele that kindled these fires!" Her spectacular
act converted many Pele devotees and advanced
Christianity in all the islands.

In far-off England, Alfred Lord Tennyson was
inspired to write in praise of her courage. In 1825
Robert Dampier, artist of the ship *Blonde*, commanded
by Lord Byron (cousin of the poet), made a sketch in
his journal of the Kilauea crater and marked with
an X the spot where a hut had been erected for
Kapiolani's use.

KAPIOLANI···
THE CHIEFESS WHO THREW ROCKS
AT A GODDESS

26 The lovers' half-flower

HAWAII'S MYSTERIOUS HALF-FLOWER NAMED NAUPAKA is both a botanical curiosity and a legend. Many stories are told of its romantic origin, as it symbolizes parted lovers.

One tale concerns a girl named Puna who became angry with her lover. She took a *naupaka* flower, which legend says was then a whole blossom, tore it in half and declared that until her lover brought her a new whole blossom she would never see him again. When Puna tore the *naupaka*, the gods changed all the blossoms of the Hawaiian Islands to half-flowers which continue to grow in incomplete form to this day. It is said the young man searched in vain for a single whole flower and died of a broken heart, leaving Puna to regret her outburst of temper.

In another story, two youthful Hawaiian lovers of such divided social classes that they could not hope to marry resolved to die together, but the gods disapproved, turning the girl's spirit into the *naupaka* of the beach, while the boy's became the *naupaka* of the mountains. It is believed that if a beach half-flower is paired with a mountain half-flower, the spirits of these young lovers are united. When two half-flowers are pressed together they resemble a "normal blossom," the whole *naupaka* of Hawaiian myth.

NAUPAKA
HAWAII'S HALF-FLOWER

ACTUAL SIZE
OF BLOSSOM

RAY
LANTERMAN

27 Featherwork of ruling chiefs

EACH ISLAND GROUP OF POLYNESIA DEVELOPED A
notable art of one kind or another—in New Zealand
it was wood sculpture, in Easter Island it was stone
image making, while in Hawaii it was featherwork.
This grand art is the spectacular peak of Hawaiian
craft, symbolic of the Hawaiian aristocracy. The cloaks
and helmets of Hawaiian ruling chiefs showed both
their rank and supreme confidence in their high position
in relation to the gods from whom they claimed
descent. Red feathers represented the gods in most of
Polynesia, so red was a color no commoner would
dare to wear. Yellow, the second dominant color of
Hawaiian featherwork, was also highly sacred.

A feather supply required skillful professional
fowlers who caught small birds of certain species
(*'i'iwi*, *'apapane*, *'o'o* and *mamo*) with lime, snares or
nets. Some birds, the *mamo* was one, were plucked of
certain feathers, then released to grow more. The
feathers were tied in small bundles and fixed into the
network fabric of the garment.

It is estimated that a yellow cloak of Kamehameha
I, now in the Bernice P. Bishop Museum, Honolulu,
contains 450,000 feathers from 80,000 birds. Feathers
were used on cloaks, capes and helmets, as coverings
of war gods, as headbands, leis and ceremonial wands
called *kahili*.

80,000 BIRDS
CONTRIBUTED 450,000 FEATHERS
TO MAKE THE SPLENDID YELLOW CLOAK
FOR KAMEHAMEHA I.

THE CLOAK CONSISTS ALMOST ENTIRELY OF
PLUMAGE FROM THE *MAMO*: EACH BIRD
POSSESSED BUT A HALF-
DOZEN SUITABLE
FEATHERS

OTHER BRILLIANT HAWAIIAN BIRDS WHOSE FEATHERS
WERE USED IN CLOAKS, CAPES AND HELMETS:

O'O
YELLOW FEATHERS

I'IWI
RED FEATHERS

APAPANE

RAY
LANTERMAN

28 Whalers and Asian junks

As WHALING DECLINED IN THE ATLANTIC OCEAN THE whalers of New England moved into the Pacific in the 1790's, followed by the ships of other nations. These whalemen combed the seas off the coasts of Chile, Peru, Japan and Northwest America, and the Arctic Ocean. The Hawaiian Islands served as a natural port of supply, refuge and recreation for the crews in winter.

By 1844 four to five hundred whaling ships were anchored off Honolulu and Lahaina, Maui, and the crews often went ashore on sprees. They posed a problem for the missionaries who wished to protect their flocks. Grog and gambling, women and the brawls of sailors relaxing from long months at sea did not make a pretty picture, yet whaling brought economic prosperity to Hawaii until about 1870.

Ships of another kind had arrived in Hawaiian waters from time to time before the coming of Captain Cook. They were Asian junks, disabled at sea and then carried by the North Pacific current to Hawaii. From such drifters the Hawaiians no doubt got their small amounts of metals and knowledge of a culture different from their own. In 1839 the whaleship *James Loper* rescued a Japanese boat in Hawaiian waters with seven crew members alive after drifting five months. They had gold and silver on board; however, they were put ashore in Honolulu without charge.

66

EAST MEETS WEST
IN HAWAIIAN WATERS

29 How Captain Cook died a god

CAPTAIN JAMES COOK WAS UNWITTINGLY MADE A GOD
by the Hawaiians who later killed him. It happened
in this way: in January, 1778, while his ships were
sailing north from Tahiti to search for a passage above
America into the Atlantic Ocean, the Hawaiian
Islands were discovered. Oahu was sighted first, then
Kauai, where a landing was made at Waimea. There
the Hawaiians saw their first Europeans. Cook sailed
north in his search, then returned to Hawaii and
anchored in Kealakekua Bay for refreshment.

According to legend, this cove was sacred to Lono,
who had left Hawaii in ancient times, promising to
return. The annual *makahiki* festival honoring Lono
was in progress. The sails of Cook's vessels resembled
the white bark-cloth standards of Lono. Hawaiian
priests thought Cook must be Lono. When he obligingly
submitted to temple ceremonies, they were convinced.

Relationships remained friendly although the
Hawaiians stole things and sailors broke tabus. The
scene was set for trouble. The ships sailed away, but a
kona or south wind storm which damaged the
Resolution forced their return. This time they were
unwelcome, especially since their food was exhausted
and the festival season ended. Following the theft of
a ship's cutter, Cook went ashore to take as hostage
against the return of the boat the ruling chief
Kalaniopuu. A fight ensued, and Cook was killed and
his bones divided as relics among the chiefs who asked
Captain Clerke, Cook's successor, "When will Lono
return?" In Polynesia gods could die, then be reborn.

SQUARE SAILS... AND MISTAKEN IDENTITY

CAPTAIN JAMES COOK, R.N.
FROM A PORTRAIT BY WEBBER. CA.1776

APPEARING SUDDENLY FROM THE
GREAT UNKNOWN, THE SAILS OF
CAPTAIN COOK'S SHIPS SO RESEMBLED
THE BANNER OF THE GOD *LONO* THAT
COOK WAS ASSUMED TO BE LONO
IN PERSON, FULFILLING THE
PROPHECY OF HIS RETURN

LONO'S BANNER WAS CARRIED ABOUT BY PRIESTS AT FESTIVALS
-- AND AT TAX-GATHERING TIME, AS SHOWN HERE

RAY LANTERMAN

30 Ukulele and 'ukeke

THE HAWAIIANS HAD MANY UNUSUAL INSTRUMENTS, AND music was always a part of their daily life as it is today. Some old-style instruments are still used, and Western instruments have been adapted. The ukulele is as Hawaiian as the Hawaiians, yet this was not always so. Like pineapples, it is a foreign import.

Small instruments called *'ukeke,* made of a narrow strip of wood 15 to 24 inches long, over which were stretched two or three strings of coconut fiber, were used by the ancient Hawaiians. One end of the *'ukeke* was held between the lips so the mouth acted as a resonance chamber when the strings were plucked. A skillful player could form words, and the *'ukeke* was a favorite love-making instrument which could express thoughts of a lover to his beloved.

The ukulele is not related to the *'ukeke,* though the name is similar and both are stringed instruments of about the same length. The ukulele is a Hawaiian adaptation of a small type of guitar which originated in Portugal. It is said that a João Gomes de Silva had one of these instruments in his possession when he went to Honolulu in 1879 aboard the sailing ship *Ravenscraig.* A fellow passenger on the ship named João Fernandez played it before Hawaiians with such a lively style that the Hawaiians called this little guitar a "ukulele" or "jumping flea," after the quick strum and mannerisms of Mr. Fernandez. The Hawaiians made their own versions of the ukulele. In time it became Hawaii's most popular instrument.

31 Kamehameha: Hawaii's first king

KAMEHAMEHA THE GREAT IS THE MOST SPECTACULAR figure in Hawaiian history. Before his birth, about 1755, a prophecy foretold the child would become "a killer of chiefs and ruler of all the islands." The ruling chief Alapai demanded the baby be killed the moment it was born, so the mother fled to the mountains of Kohala, Hawaii, where the young child Kamehameha could be safe. His name, meaning "the lonely one," commemorates his early seclusion.

As a young man Kamehameha went aboard the ships of Captain James Cook in 1779 in Kealakekua Bay and saw firearms and Western trade practice which he later adopted to his own use. Hawaii was then ruled by four major chiefs who were antagonistic to one another. Kamehameha resolved to unify the islands and achieved his aim in founding a kingdom in 1795, and completed unification in 1810. He was a ferocious and ruthless warrior but in peace a wise and capable administrator much loved by his people.

He had several wives, two of whom are well remembered. The first, his sacred wife Keopuolani, who produced heirs of highest rank, was restraining company as Kamehameha was of lower birth and obliged to observe uncomfortable tabus when near her. His favorite wife was Queen Kaahumanu, a brilliant and intelligent woman who stayed with him when foreign visitors were present.

King Kamehameha died in 1819 and was buried in secret according to ancient customs.

THE LONELY ONE
· KAMEHAMEHA ·
FIRST KING OF ALL THE ISLANDS

HIS FAVORITE WIFE
KAAHUMANU

FROM PORTRAITS BY CHORIS

HIS WARS OF CONQUEST WERE FEARSOME AFFAIRS
AND HIS PERSONAL WAR GOD *KUKAILIMOKU*
WAS CARRIED INTO BATTLE BY THE HIGH PRIEST
TO INSPIRE THE TROOPS AND TO STRIKE
TERROR INTO THE ENEMY.

RAY
LANTERMAN

32 The ancient art of petroglyphs

ONE OF THE MOST FASCINATING OF HAWAIIAN ARTS IS that of petroglyphs, inscribed stone pictures of animals, men, geometric forms, and mysterious symbols. Pictures cut on lava surfaces are found throughout the Hawaiian Islands. They were the writing of old Hawaii.

Rock pictures are found on trails, at camp sites, near landing points and in isolated places. Various lava rocks were used, but the flat ones were favored. Cliff or cave walls, smooth boulders and sandstone shelves also served this mysterious art.

It is easy to identify most of these rock drawings, as the subjects are simple, yet some are obscure. Whether they had ritual significance or were mere doodling is a question that has never been adequately answered. They probably had both sacred and secular uses. The appearance of European ships, guns, horses and letters in Hawaiian petroglyphic art indicates such were made after European contact, while the earliest date back many centuries.

These rock pictures were formed by pecking away at the lava surface with a small hard stone to form lines about half an inch wide. Those wishing to follow the mysterious trail of petroglyphic pictures should visit the island of Hawaii, which offers the most numerous groups and greatest diversity of style.

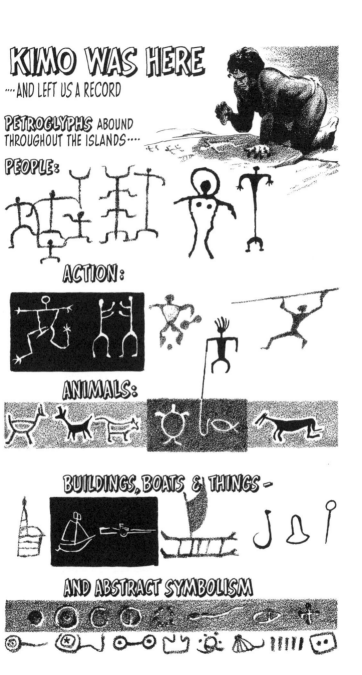

KIMO WAS HERE

···AND LEFT US A RECORD

PETROGLYPHS ABOUND
THROUGHOUT THE ISLANDS····

PEOPLE:

ACTION:

ANIMALS:

BUILDINGS, BOATS & THINGS –

AND ABSTRACT SYMBOLISM

33 The first written Hawaiian

THE HAWAIIAN LANGUAGE BELONGS TO THE POLYNESIAN
family of languages with which it shares a typical
rich musical quality. It is a language of poetic feeling,
ideal for expressing emotions in song, or saying things
in the softest possible manner. It was not readily
rendered into Western letters and lost much in the
process of becoming a written language.

Captain James Cook collected a short Hawaiian
vocabulary. A list of 250 words appears in his Journal,
but no one had attempted to write the whole language
before the coming of the New England missionary
party which arrived in 1820. In committee they fixed
on certain letters for the sounds of an alien speech,
namely the Hawaiian language which belongs to the
Malayo-Polynesian language family. The more
scholarly of the missionaries read Greek and Hebrew;
however, the grammar and the orthography which
they adopted did not exactly represent the Hawaiian
language. Yet they did well under the circumstances.
Hawaiian sounds simple when it is in fact subtle. The
vowels are all pronounced as in Italian, and seven
consonants (h, k, l, m, n, p, w) are fixed on in modern
written Hawaiian. The 'r' and 't' sounds, commonly
used in the time of Captain Cook and throughout the
missionary period in some districts, survive on the
island of Ni'ihau.

In spite of many difficulties in rendering the
Hawaiian language, Elisha Loomis in 1822 printed a
Hawaiian-English speller which was Hawaii's first
locally produced book.

A a	â	as in *father*,	la—sun.
E e	a	— *fete*,	hemo—cast off.
I i	e	— *marine*,	marie—quiet.
O o	o	— *over*,	
U u	oo	— *rule*,	

CONSONANTS.	*Names.*	CONSONANTS.	
b	be	N n	
d	de		

34 A way of escape in old Hawaii

TABU LAWS CALLED KAPU HEDGED IN OLD-TIME Hawaiians. To break a *kapu* incurred a death sentence if one was caught. *Kapu* justice was swift and summary if the offender was a commoner or a slave. A second hazard, even to the innocent, was to be on the losing side in time of war. Those captured were usually exterminated, or at best made slaves. In either event the only hope was to reach a place of refuge before being apprehended. Certain temples were known sanctuaries offering protection if the fleeing person could get through the gate. Pursuers could not enter.

Once the fleeing person was inside a refuge the spirits of the dead provided protection, backed by priests. Those defeated in war were received and protected by priests while tabu breakers could be purified by rituals.

Hawaii had many such temples. The most famous, preserved to this day, is on the edge of Honaunau Bay, Hawaii; it was built by Kona's ruling chiefs who lived about the mid-16th century. Hawaii's most spectacular "stone-age" monument, it occupies a site of about six acres and is surrounded by stone walls averaging 17 feet in width and 10 feet in height. This "City of Refuge," or more correctly, this "Place of Refuge," is a National Historical Park. How many men, women and children entered its gate to find safety or died in a vain attempt to reach its sanctuary, will never be known.

ONCE YOU WERE INSIDE, THEY COULDN'T TOUCH YOU

WHATEVER MISCHIEF A PERSON MAY HAVE BEEN UP TO, IF HE COULD MAKE IT THROUGH THE GATES OF A CITY OF REFUGE, HE WAS SAFE FROM RETRIBUTION

FUGITIVES AND REFUGEES WERE SHELTERED IN GRASS HOUSES, AND A HIEAU WAS NEARBY, WHERE RITES OF ABSOLUTION WERE CONDUCTED

RAY LANTERMAN

35 Diamond Head: symbol of Hawaii

HAWAII'S GIBRALTAR IS A MAJESTIC VOLCANIC CONE overlooking Waikiki, some 760 feet high and about 300,000 years old. It has captured the imagination of visitors to Hawaii from the 18th century to the present time. Mark Twain said Diamond Head was the most stirring sight he had ever seen.

The Hawaiians called Diamond Head "Leahi" which means Place of Fire or possibly "brow of the *ahi* fish." In 1792 John Sykes, first mate under Captain George Vancouver, sketched Diamond Head as "Point of Whytete Bay, Woohoo." The old spellings for Waikiki and Oahu are recognizable. Earlier, in 1786, Captain Portlock had called this impressive sentinel "Point Rose." By whatever name, Diamond Head commands the coast about Honolulu and has been an important fortress.

The name Diamond Head originated when roving sailors found on the slopes calcite crystals which some people call "Pele's diamonds." Sparkling in the sun, these crystals deceived the sailors who thought they had found diamonds. Kamehameha then made the crater tabu until John Young, his European advisor, told him the crystals were worthless.

On the western slopes of Diamond Head on the site of the La Pietra mansion (now The Hawaii School for Girls) stood a stone temple, *heiau*, where Kamehameha I and his predecessors made bloody sacrifice to the God of War.

We're RICH!
SHOUTED THE SAILORS
AND DIAMOND HEAD GOT ITS NAME
RAY LANTERMAN

36 Oahu's miraculous water system

PURE WATER WAS SCARCE IN OLD HAWAII FOR THOSE who lived away from springs or streams. Hawaiians often drank brackish water and endured its bacteria by acquired immunities; however, early European travellers found the same water loosened their bowels and gave them fevers.

For a thousand years the Hawaiians sat unknowingly on vast reservoirs of fresh water. Twentieth-century science used geographical, hydrographical and engineering skills to tap water resources, and the dense populations of Honolulu and Waikiki became possible.

Huge subterranean artesian basins exist under those Hawaiian islands which have rain-catching mountains. Ocean evaporation forms humid, cloud-laden air that the northeast trades carry over the islands. Some of the moisture is condensed as rain when the warm wet air is pushed upwards into colder regions by mountain barriers. As rain falls on high areas, water is absorbed and filtered down through vertical dikes of porous lava rock which in turn feed subterranean "lenses" of fresh water which stand both above and below sea level. Even when these reservoirs extend below sea level, they remain fresh because fresh water mixes with salt water only along the margins. Some obstructed dikes break out on hillsides, making springs. Skilled engineers of the Board of Water Supply tap Oahu's remarkable sources of pure water for the island residents and the millions of tourists who visit Waikiki each year.

HE WAI E OLA
WATER FOR LIFE

WHERE HONOLULU'S FRESH WATER COMES FROM ···
··· THE 'LENS' ··· HOW IT WORKS

RAIN — FRESH WATER LENS — CAP ROCK

SEA LEVEL

SALT WATER SEEPAGE FROM OCEAN

ZONE OF SALT WATER — FRESH/SALT MIXTURE

FRESH/SALT

1 AN ISLAND WITHOUT RAIN HAS NO FRESH WATER SUPPLY

2 RAIN WATER FILTERS DOWN THROUGH ISLAND'S ROCK AND COLLECTS IN A LENS-SHAPE, FLOATING ON THE HEAVIER SALT WATER

3 AS ISLAND ERODES, ACCUMULATED CAP ROCK SEALS OFF OCEAN WATER AND LENS GROWS LARGER

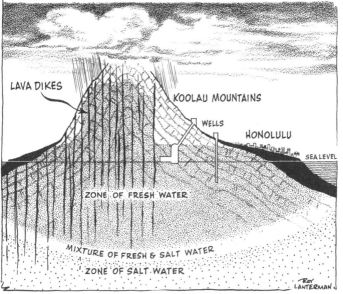

LAVA DIKES

KOOLAU MOUNTAINS

WELLS

HONOLULU

SEA LEVEL

ZONE OF FRESH WATER

MIXTURE OF FRESH & SALT WATER

ZONE OF SALT WATER

ROY LANTERMAN

37 A love marriage of princess and commoner

PRINCESS BERNICE PAUAHI WAS BORN AT HONOLULU on a stormy December day in 1831 to High Chief Abner Paki and aristocratic Konia. As a great granddaughter of King Kamehameha, she was of high nobility. The man she married in 1850, Charles Reed Bishop, then collector general of customs in Honolulu, was born in 1822 in a toll house where his father was keeper, at Glens Falls, N. Y. Charles Reed was soon orphaned, and the prospects in life seemed dismal for this infant; yet he was to become Hawaii's banker and would marry a beautiful Hawaiian princess.

This marriage was the fruit of strong love and determination, as Princess Pauahi's parents opposed the marriage for reasons which seemed obvious. In fact, they refused to attend the wedding. Except for the absence of children the marriage proved successful. Princess Pauahi and her husband were both of high character, humble and benevolent. Called to the deathbed of King Kamehameha V, to whom she had been informally betrothed as a girl, Princess Pauahi declined his wish that she succeed him on the throne.

She was determined to serve her Hawaiian people in other ways. With her husband she helped in the founding of Queen's Hospital and worked for the welfare and education of Hawaiians until her death. Her vast estate went to the continuance and advancement of Kamehameha Schools. The famous Bernice P. Bishop Museum was established in her memory by her husband, Charles Reed Bishop, in 1889.

84

THE COUPLE WHO CARED

THE PRINCESS BERNICE PAUAHI AND HER HUSBAND, CHARLES REED BISHOP, FROM A DAGUERREOTYPE TAKEN SOON AFTER THEIR WEDDING

38 Hawaii and its many flowers

THE BLOSSOMS OF HAWAII ARE OF MANY ORIGINS AND
whether indigenous or imported, many have symbolical
meanings. The hibiscus which grows in many hues and
sizes is the official flower of the State of Hawaii. All
islands have their own official flower. These are:
Hawaii, the red *lehua* (*ohiʻa*); Maui, the *lokelani* (pink
cottage rose); Molokai, the white *kukui* blossom;
Kahoolawe, the *hinahina* (beach heliotrope); Lanai,
the *kaunaʻoa* (yellow and orange air plant); Oahu, the
ʻilima; and Kauai, the *mokihana* (green berry). Niʻihau
has the white *pupu* shell as its symbol.

The commonest flower of the Islands is the plumeria,
very popular as a lei flower because of its beauty and
abundance. The delicate flowers vary in color from
white through yellow, coral, pink and red.

The plumeria was introduced to Hawaii from
tropical America and became abundant in cemeteries.
Although it is widely worn in leis today, conservative
old-timers would not wear this flower because they
considered it disrespectful to the dead as well as an
invitation to trouble from the unseen world. In old
Hawaii the spirits of the dead were thought to watch
the acts and affairs of the living very closely.

FROM
GRAVEYARD
TREE
TO
GRACIOUS
GIFT

RAY
LANTERMAN

39 Famous literary visitors

HAWAIIAN LITERATURE WAS BORN WHEN CAPTAIN James Cook recorded his discovery of the Hawaiian Islands one fateful day in January, 1778. An English-language literature has overlaid the rich oral tradition of the Hawaiians, which has in part been written down to become Hawaii's aboriginal literature.

The explorers' journals of the 18th century and later journals, letters and diaries of missionaries and others laid the foundation of a Western literary tradition. From 1778 to the present, a period of about 200 years, Hawaii has gained an enormous literature which has its shining lights in writers of international fame who had only briefly visited, either in the late 19th or early 20th century. The most famous literary names are: Richard Henry Dana, Jr. (1815–1882); Herman Melville (1819–1891); Samuel Langhorne Clemens—better known as Mark Twain (1835–1910); Robert Louis Stevenson (1850–1894); and Jack London (1876–1916). All were Americans with the exception of Robert Louis Stevenson of Scotland.

All were affected by the charm of Hawaii and its hospitalities, except Herman Melville who saw Honolulu at a time when the impact of Western culture was showing its worst effects. Other great literary visitors of later years included Rupert Brooke, Charles Nordhoff, Somerset Maugham. Strangely, none mentioned made Hawaii his home.

88

HAWAII'S IMPRESSION ON SOME
FAMOUS AUTHORS

ONCE HE WAS STRAIGHT ON JUST WHERE THEY'RE LOCATED, MARK TWAIN LIKED THE *SANDWICH ISLANDS*... BUT HE WAS A LITTLE PERTURBED BY THE NUMBER OF CATS HE FOUND.

JACK LONDON WONDERED HOW MANY TIMES KALANIKUPULE'S SOLDIERS BUMPED AS THEY FELL HEADLONG OVER THE PALI.

TUSITALA ··· The Story-Teller: ROBERT LOUIS STEVENSON, INTIMATE FRIEND OF KING KALAKAUA AND THE PRINCESS KAIULANI, WORKED IN A DILAPIDATED WAIKIKI SHACK WHICH HE SHARED WITH CENTIPEDES, SPIDERS AND LIZARDS.

"Heaven help the islands of the sea," WAILED THE AUTHOR OF *MOBY DICK*. HERMAN MELVILLE WAS NOT AT ALL IMPRESSED WITH THE HONOLULU OF HIS DAY. HE TOOK ISSUE WITH THE CONDUCT OF THE MISSIONARIES, FOUND THE MERCHANTS DISINTERESTED, AND WROTE DISPARAGINGLY OF THE KING.

IN HIS CLASSIC *TWO YEARS BEFORE THE MAST*, DANA SPEAKS WARMLY OF THE *SANDWICH ISLANDERS* HE MET IN CALIFORNIA. SOME 24 YEARS LATER HE VISITED HAWAII —
...that most fascinating group of islands."

RAY LANTERMAN

40 Paniolo and the pa'u riders

IN HAWAIIAN PARADES, ESPECIALLY THE KAMEHAMEHA
Day parade in June each year in Honolulu, glimpses
of Hawaii's romantic history can be seen in the
cavalcades of the Hawaiian paniolo from many cattle
ranches and their graceful companions, the pa'u
riders. The long trailing skirts of these horsewomen
originated as utilitarian waist wraps or *pa'u,* used to
protect dresses on dusty roads and trails.

The significant paniolo or cowboy history began in
1832 when King Kamehameha III imported a number
of Spanish-Mexican vaqueros from California to
round up the cattle descended from those left on the
island of Hawaii by Captain George Vancouver in
1794, and to teach his people their trade. Lacking a
name for them, the Hawaiians adopted the Spanish
word paniolo which derives from the word *español,*
meaning Spanish. So this word came to be applied to
range riders of Hawaii.

The Hawaiians adopted colonial Spanish saddles,
dress and music. The slack-key guitar tuning became
a unique kind of Hawaiian music. The Hawaiian
paniolo is as dashing and colorful a cowboy as any of
those seen in Western movies.

PANIOLOS...

AND
PA'U
RIDERS

RAY
LANTERMAN

41 Old Ironsides visits Honolulu

HAWAII HAS SEEN MANY FAMOUS SHIPS, MOST OF WHICH achieved fame in the Pacific. For example, there was Captain James Cook's H.M.S. *Resolution* which sailed with the H.M.S. *Discovery* into Hawaiian waters in 1778.

A fascinating fact which has escaped Hawaiian history books is the visit of the U.S.S. *Constitution* ("Old Ironsides") which anchored off Honolulu in 1845. Launched in 1797, this wonderful frigate saw service in the Atlantic and survives to this day as a historic museum ship on the East Coast.

The Hawaiian visit of "Old Ironsides" is recorded by editor James Jackson Jarves in the Honolulu newspaper *Polynesian*, November 22, 1845. Here are his words: "U.S. Frigate *Constitution*, Capt. Percival, anchored in our waters on Sunday, the 16th, and next morning at 8 o'clock exchanged salutes with the fort. The *Constitution* is well known by the sobriquet of "Old Ironsides" from the good service she did in the late war between the U. S. and Great Britain, having captured the frigates *Java* and *Guerrière*, and sloops *Cyane* and *Levant*. She has always been a lucky ship and the associations connected with her history make her the pride of the American Navy."

Hawaii was honored by the visit of this distinguished ship. As the 50th State of America there is a special patriotic reason for remembering the visit of "Old Ironsides" which played such a vital role in establishing American sea power.

A MOST DISTINGUISHED VISITOR

OLD IRONSIDES OFF DIAMOND HEAD

42 The upside-down falls of Nu'uanu valley

TOURISTS WHO COME TO OAHU USUALLY SEE AT LEAST something of the verdant Nu'uanu Valley which reaches from Honolulu to the famous Pali. Not many see the "upside-down falls" there, as their play occurs only in certain weather conditions.

The name Nu'uanu means "cool height." Before the spread of houses with their gardens, and forestation efforts, the upper height of the valley was a barren windswept pass to the windward side.

In 1795 King Kamehameha I pursued the warriors of Oahu to the abrupt end of Nu'uanu Valley, called the Pali. Here the retreating remnants of the local defenders of unknown numbers died in a last stand, some being pushed over the cliffs, others jumping to their deaths.

The steep ridges of the Ko'olau terminate abruptly on the eastern side of the upper valley in ravines which, after heavy rains, spout torrents that are caught by trade winds to form plumes of spray that disperse in upward flying mist. These are the upside-down falls of Nu'uanu, known to the Hawaiians as Waipuhia, or "blown water," a scenic, never-to-be-forgotten wonder.

43 Skiing in Hawaii
on real snow

THE HAWAIIAN ISLANDS WOULD SEEM THE LAST PLACE
on earth to go skiing as there appears to be about as
much chance of finding snow as there is in the Sahara
desert. But in places Hawaii does have snow.

Skiing is an established sport with several hundred
enthusiasts. Their ski ground is on the slopes of Mt.
Mauna Kea, on the Big Island. The highest point in
the Pacific world, it reaches 13,796 feet above sea
level. When measured from its base on the sea floor,
it rises 32,000 feet, which tops Mt. Everest as a
mountain mass by two or three thousand feet.

During winter, snow falls on Mauna Kea and its
twin peak Mauna Loa. In 1937 a determined group
of skiers of the Hilo Ski Club traveled up to the 7,000-
foot level, then climbed to the snowy slopes, skis and
all, but today jeeps take skiers close to snow areas.
In 1953 and thereafter the Honolulu Ski Club has
made venturesome trips to these high ski fields. Each
February the Ski Association of Hawaii has its annual
ski meet.

In Hawaii scientists and skiers share the world's
biggest mountain. The ski buffs go through their
maneuvers just below the world's highest permanent
astronomical observatory. A weather station encrusted
with ice in winter months, the Mauna Kea Observatory with its 88-inch reflector telescope stands some
two and a half miles above the Pacific Ocean and
provides valuable data on weather and the heavens.

RAY
LANTERMAN

SCIENTIST AND **SKIER**
SHARE THE WORLD'S BIGGEST MOUNTAIN ···
ON *MAUNA KEA*, SKI BUFFS SCHUSS AND TURN IN THE SHADOW OF
THE HIGHEST PERMANENT ASTRONOMICAL OBSERVATORY ON EARTH

44 The state bird is a goose

THE HAWAIIAN GOOSE, CALLED NENE BY THE HAWAIIANS and *Nesochen sandwichensis* by scientists, of the duck, goose and swan family, is indigenous to Hawaii. It arrived thousands of years ago and adapted itself to the harsh lava terrain. Its webbed feet became clawlike, able to grasp the lava surface, while its wings became modified to short flight. Before the arrival of the Hawaiians it had no predators.

This exceptional bird is not widespread in Hawaii. Even in ancient times it was confined to the islands of Hawaii and Maui although odd birds struggled ashore on other islands. The Hawaiians caught and ate the *nene* but it was firearms, indiscriminate hunting and introduced animals which brought it to near extinction. The rehabilitation of this beautiful goose is in part due to its being raised in captivity, then released in sanctuaries in the crater of Haleakala on Maui and on the mountain slopes of Mauna Loa on Hawaii. It is protected by law. The introduced mongoose eats *nene* eggs and young and thus endangers the survival of this bird. Its nest is no more than an unprotected hollow in the ground, often in areas which are grazed over by cattle and wild goats.

Many indigenous birds of Hawaii are extinct but the *nene* seems destined to continue because it is easily domesticated or held in zoos. The Honolulu Zoo has several *nene*.

45 The candlenut tree

THE KUKUI OR CANDLENUT TREE, ALEURITES MOLUCCANA, must have been brought into Polynesia from Asia by early voyagers, yet some think it is indigenous to the area. It is a tree with many uses. It is the nut that gives it the common name "candlenut tree." A dozen or more kernels of *kukui* nuts strung on the midrib of a coconut frond provided a clear burning light which lasted at the rate of one nut every two or three minutes.

The delicate flower of the candlenut tree is the symbol of the island of Molokai. The silvery green foliage is seen on the hillsides among the darker greens as shimmering frosted areas on many Hawaiian hillsides and valleys.

The nut kernels served the Hawaiians as a relish to food when roasted and ground. Uncooked, the kernel was used as medicine while the extracted oil made an excellent wood dressing. One ancient use for *kukui* nuts which has become fashionable in modern times is jewelry. The nuts are polished in their natural form, or first faceted by grinding, then polished. The *kukui* lei may be worn by both men and women and is especially appropriate for festive occasions. The natural oil which Hawaiians used in stone lamps with bark-cloth wicks was tried for early export as a lubricant and paint vehicle, but the trade did not flourish.

THE VERSATILE KUKUI

AS THE *Candlenut*, KUKUI TORCHES ILLUMINATED NIGHT-TIME ACTIVITIES

A LEI OF MATCHED KUKUI NUTS IS A TREASURED POSSESSION

BLOSSOM

DOUBLES OFTEN OCCUR

THE OIL, RUBBED INTO WOOD, IMPARTS A FINE SATINY SHEEN

POLISHED NUT
AVERAGE ACTUAL SIZE

SMALL WONDER THAT THE KUKUI IS HAWAII'S STATE TREE

RAY LANTERMAN

46 America's only royal palace

IOLANI PALACE WAS COMPLETED IN 1882 FOR KING
David Kalakaua and Queen Kapiolani. They preferred
to live in a cozier house, but used the palace for all
formal and ceremonial occasions. When King Kalakaua
died in 1891 he was succeeded by his sister Lydia
Liliuokalani, who occupied the palace. She was to
play a tragic role, for she was deposed in 1893 and
suffered confinement as a prisoner, first in her home,
Washington Place, then in the palace.

Iolani Palace remained the seat of Hawaii's governments that followed the monarchy: namely, the
provisional, republic, territorial and State governments.
After the completion of the new State Capitol in 1968,
Iolani Palace became a historic monument of great
visitor interest as the only royal palace in the U.S.A.

Translated, Iolani means "Bird of Heaven" or, more
specifically, "royal or heavenly hawk." It is a sacred
name of mystical significance.

This is indeed a sacred place. In the grounds stands
the site of the royal crypt where Hawaii's royal dead
were entombed from 1825 until 1865, when the coffins
were removed to the Royal Mausoleum in Nu'uanu
Valley.

Formerly the west gate was used for ordinary
official business, the east gate was reserved for the
royal family, the front gate was opened for State
occasions, while troops, tradesmen and retainers
entered by the back gate.

a CROWN, a THRONE, a ROYAL PALACE in AMERICA?

YES...
IN HAWAII.

BEHIND A *KAPU* STICK AND
FLANKED BY FEATHER *KAHILIS*:
THE *ONLY* ROYAL THRONE IN
THE UNITED STATES

IN THIS SKETCH FROM A PHOTOGRAPH MADE SHORTLY AFTER ITS *COMPLETION*,
IOLANI PALACE LOOKS MUCH THE SAME AS IT DOES TODAY

RAY
LANTERMAN

47 Insignia of the 50th state

VISITORS TO THE 50TH STATE ARE OFTEN SURPRISED to see the Union Jack of Britain flying on the trade winds. The Jack with eight horizontal red, white and blue stripes is Hawaii's State Flag. Each stripe represents a major island of the State.

Of the several stories of the origin of this flag, the most probable is that in 1816 King Kamehameha I wished to send his 16-gun war vessel, the *Forester*, to China with sandalwood. He had no national flag, so his British advisors, John Young and Isaac Davis, with the ship's captain, Alexander Adams, designed one. This handsome flag is the result. It has endured throughout the Hawaiian monarchy and the eras as a republic and territory of the United States, and in 1959 it became the official flag of the 50th State.

The great seal of Hawaii was adopted in 1959 by the State Legislature after serving previous governments. It bears the State motto *"Ua mau ke ea o ka aina i ka pono,"* meaning "The life of the land is perpetuated in righteousness." These words were first spoken by King Kamehameha III in 1843 when the British Admiral, Richard Thomas, countermanded the order by his countryman, Captain George Paulet, to seize the Hawaiian kingdom.

The Coat of Arms, designed in London, was adopted in 1845. It has seen many changes, the most remarkable being the substitution of an ermine drape for the feather cape.

104

48 Two royal songwriters

Song and chant were important to the ancient Hawaiians, who had no writing. Song, like hula, had both sacred and secular functions, while composition has always been an aristocratic avocation.

The royal composers, King David Kalakaua, 1874 to 1891, and his sister, Queen Liliuokalani, Hawaii's last monarch, 1891 to 1893, gave Hawaii some of its most loved songs.

King Kalakaua composed words for the anthem *Hawaii Pono'i* ("Hawaii's Own"). It served the kingdom and territory periods of Hawaii, then became the anthem of the 50th State. The royal bandmaster, Captain Henri Berger, wrote the music. King Kalakaua, the builder of Iolani Palace and bearer of the nickname "The Merry Monarch," was as good at composing drinking songs as he was at writing songs of patriotism.

Queen Liliuokalani was the most gifted of all Hawaiian composers of the 19th century. She excelled in writing love songs. *Aloha 'Oe* ("Farewell to You"), the best known of her compositions, was inspired by two lovers she saw in tender embrace before parting. Although a farewell for lovers, this song is now an international farewell still played at its best in Hawaii.

THE ORIGINAL INSPIRATION FOR
QUEEN LILIUOKALANI'S
HAUNTING *"Aloha Oe"* IS SAID TO
HAVE COME TO HER AS SHE WATCHED
TWO LOVERS PARTING AT
NUUANU PALI

Musical Monarchs

KING KALAKAUA

THE "MERRY MONARCH" HAS A LONG
LIST OF SONG TITLES TO HIS CREDIT;
AMONG THEM: *Pili Aoao, Kokohi,
Ninipo, Sweet Lei Lehua* and
Koni Au I Ka Wai.

HE ALSO WROTE THE WORDS FOR
HAWAII'S ANTHEM *Hawaii Ponoi*

RAY
LANTERMAN

49 Oahu's most sacred burial place

THE KINGS, QUEENS AND NOBLES OF THE KAMEHAMEHA
and Kalakaua dynasties and others of importance in
Hawaiian history lie at rest in the Royal Mausoleum
situated just north of downtown Honolulu in lower
Nu'uanu Valley. This plot of ground is the most
sacred of places to Hawaiians. Visitors there should
respect the ground they walk on.

The first Royal Mausoleum on Oahu was built to
receive the bones of the noble dead on Iolani Palace
grounds in 1825. It was prepared to receive the bodies
of King Kamehameha II and Queen Kamamalu,
both of whom died in England. This old site in the
southeast corner of the palace grounds is marked by a
mound surrounded by an iron railing and *ti* plants.

When the new mausoleum was completed in
Nu'uanu Valley in 1865, 18 coffins of kings,
queens and nobles were transferred from the old
crypt, including two remarkable coconut sennit caskets
allegedly containing the bones of the ancient rulers
Liloa and Lonoikamakahi. These unique caskets were
later transferred to the Bernice P. Bishop Museum
for scientific study and conservation.

Marked burial places were not popular with the
ancient Hawaiians, as enemies delighted in insulting
a dead chief and his living relations by converting
his bones into fishhooks or other objects. Kamehameha
I, who was never converted to Christianity, was
buried in a secret cave somewhere on the Big Island.

ROYAL MAUSOLEUM, NUUANU VALLEY

LUNALILO'S TOMB AT
KAWAIAHAO CHURCH

ANCIENT COFFIN
OF SENNIT

RAY
LANTERMAN

50 The saga of Hawaii's shipping lanes

THE HISTORY OF THE HAWAIIAN ISLANDS IS LARGELY a story of the sea and ships. Tradition claims canoes voyaged to and from Tahiti, a belief supported by the name of the channel between Maui and Kahoolawe, Ke Ala-i-Kahiki, or "The Path to Tahiti." The era following the canoe was dominated by the European sailing ship.

Spanish galleons had made their annual Acapulco—Manila voyages across the North Pacific for over 200 years before Cook discovered Hawaii, yet there is no evidence they opened up Hawaii's sea lanes to Western culture. Trading began with Captain Cook's ships; nails were standard currency.

In the 19th century sailing vessels of missionary parties, whalers, traders and settlers came to Hawaii. The beautiful four-masted *Falls of Clyde*, docked in Honolulu as a museum ship, is an example of the last of these sailing traders. In 1882 Captain William Matson began regular passenger and freight service to Hawaii with a single ship. By 1909 four vessels flew the Matson flag, and in 1935 there were 50 ships with the blue "M" on their funnels. Airways competition in the 1960's dwindled the passenger lists, yet the sea remains Hawaii's lifeline. Consumer goods, food and fuel come by container ships and enormous tankers to make modern Hawaiian life possible.

51 The saga of air travel

PREEMINENT AS A SEAPORT IN THE MID-PACIFIC FROM
1778 when Captain Cook discovered the islands,
Hawaii today is the vital link between the North
American and Asian continents. With Pacific island
groups to its west and south, Hawaii has an enviable
advantage. Climate, convenience and its fascinating
people attract millions of tourists, most of whom come
by air. Ships are now for the leisurely few.

The saga of Hawaii's airways began December 31,
1910, when an aviator by the name of "Bud" Mars
flew his kite-like biplane from a field at Moanalua,
Oahu, close to today's major airways system where
about a thousand aircraft use the runways daily at
Honolulu International Airport.

Commercial flying began in Hawaii on November
11, 1929. Inter-Island Airways, now called Hawaiian
Airlines, then obtained two Sikorsky S-38 amphibians
which landed on the waters and were met by outrigger
canoes. Transpacific flying began in 1925 when
Commander John Rogers and his naval crew flew a
seaplane from California to Oahu. On October 22,
1936, Pan-American Airways (now Pan-American
World Airways) carried its first paying passengers to
Honolulu in boat-like Hawaii Clipper four-engined
seaplanes between San Francisco and Honolulu. The
trip took eighteen to twenty hours. Today, modern
jets fly the same route in four or five hours.

112

COFFEE, TEA OR MILK?

INTER·ISLAND

IN 1929: YOUR FLIGHT BEGAN WITH A CANOE RIDE TO THE WAITING SIKORSKY....
..... TODAY'S JETS STREAK FROM ISLAND TO ISLAND FASTER THAN YOU CAN SAY "PINEAPPLE JUICE."

MAINLAND·HAWAII

1925: JOHN RODGERS & CREW MADE IT IN ABOUT 25½ HOURS .....

HONOLULU'S HUGE JET TERMINAL IS NAMED FOR RODGERS

1927: SMITH AND BRONTE DID, TOO... BUT THEIR MOLOKAI LANDING WAS A LITTLE ROUGH

LATE 30'S-EARLY 40'S: ENORMOUS FLYING BOATS CHUGGED ACROSS THE OCEAN IN A SPEEDY 18 HOURS

RAY LANTERMAN

HAWAII·ANYWHERE ··· NOW.

A MOVIE / A SNACK / A SHORT NAP / AND YOU'RE THERE

LONDON MAURITIUS PER? CALCUTTA TELAVIV AN? ACAPULCO OSLO CHICAGO COPENHAGEN NAIROBI PANAMA NEW YORK DUB LIN LISBON LO ANGELES VIENNA TOKYO RIO DE JANEIRO SE ATTLE BERLIN S APORE BOSTON KOKOMO OMBAY BEIRUT WELLINGTON H KONG MADRID VANCOUVER TEHI ?AN SAN FRANCI MEXICO CITY APIA MANILA MONTR ANCHORAGE SYDNEY INDIANAPOLIS IMA DENVER ATHENS WASHINGTO N ROME DALLA LEBANON PARIS MINNEAPOLIS GUADALAJA RA FRANKFURT SALT LAKE CITY NANDI ISTANBUL ST LOUIS PE? ?H MIAMI AMSTERDAM GLASCOW REGINA CAPETOWN DUB UQUE MOSCOW ST CROIX ATLANTA OSAKA PORTSMOUT? ? ST PAUL STOCKHOLM ADDIS ABABA BANGOR YAZOO CITY BANKOK SPOKANE HELSINKI OAKLAND QUITO LAS VEGAS PEK

52 Hawaii's cosmopolitan people

INTERNATIONALISM IS A CHARACTERISTIC OF HAWAII'S cosmopolitan people. The landscape may be spectacular, the climate wonderful, the beaches a sheer delight, yet Hawaii's greatest charm is its people, and people-watching is a local hobby.

Hawaii's people have evolved over many centuries. Archaeologists tell us the first group arrived from the Marquesas Islands, probably in the 7th century, followed by a second wave from the Society Islands in about the mid–13th century. They lived in Hawaii for several centuries without meeting other peoples except possibly those on an odd drifting junk from Asia, or a Spanish ship. Following Captain Cook's discovery of Hawaii in 1778, whalers, traders, explorers and missionaries arrived, bringing Western diseases and a social system which the Hawaiians did not readily comprehend. The healthy population of an estimated 300,000 Hawaiians of Cook's time were by 1850 reduced to about 84,000.

In the succeeding century sugar and pineapple plantations required labor, and more than 400,000 recruits came from foreign lands. Japan and Okinawa sent 180,000, the Philippines 125,000, China 46,000, Portugal 17,500, Korea 8,000, Puerto Rico 6,000, the South Pacific 2,500, Russia 2,000, Spain 8,000 and Germany and Galicia 1,300. Americans of both African and Caucasian strains, and other races from Eskimo to Greek, intermingled their manners and genes. Widespread intermarriage has made Hawaii the true racial melting pot of the Pacific.

TUTTLE BOOKS ON HAWAII AND THE PACIFIC

ART AND HANDICRAFTS:

Art and Life in Polynesia *by Terence Barrow*

Decorative Arts of the New Zealand Maori *by Terence Barrow*

Tropical Flower Arranging: A Practical Guide *by Nancy A. Inman*

Coconut Palm Frond Weaving *by William H. Goodloe*

HISTORY:

The Hawaiians: An Island People *by Helen Gay Pratt; drawings by Rosamond S. Morgan and Juliette May Fraser*

Hawaii's Story by Hawaii's Queen *by Liliuokalani*

Calabashes and Kings: An Introduction to Hawaii *by Stanley D. Porteus*

Ancient Hawaiian Civilization: A Series of Lectures delivered at the Kamehameha Schools (revised) *by E. S. Craighill Handy and Others*

Lawrence M. Judd and Hawaii: An Autobiography *by Lawrence M. Judd as told to Hugh W. Lytle*

The Hawaiian Chief's Children's School 1839-1850 *by Mary A. Richards*

Six Months in the Sandwich Islands *by Isabella Bird*

Men From Under the Sky: The Arrival of Westerners in Fiji *by Stanley Brown*

Islands of Destiny *by Olive Wyndette*

Surfing: The Sport of Hawaiian Kings *by Ben R. Finney and James D. Houston*

Incidents of a Whaling Voyage *by Francis Allyn Olmsted*

An Account of the Polynesian Race: Its Origin and Migrations *by Abraham Fornander*

Missionary Adventures in the South Pacific *by David and Leona Crawford*

Guam Past and Present *by Charles Beardsley*

The Drama of Fiji: A Contemporary History *by Dr. John Wesley Coulter*

LANGUAGE:

Dictionary of the Hawaiian Language *by Lorrin Andrews*

An English-Hawaiian Dictionary: With Various Useful Tables *by H. R. Hitchcock*

Hawaiian Phrase Book

A Short Synopsis of the Most Essential Points in Hawaiian Grammar *by W. D. Alexander*

MANNERS AND CUSTOMS:

Myths and Legends of the Polynesians *by Johannes E. Andersen*

The Polynesian Family System in Ka-ʻu Hawaiʻi *by E. S. Craighill Handy and M. K. Pukui*

Polynesian Researches (4 Volumes) *by William Ellis*

Hawaii Goes Fishing *by Jean Scott MacKellar*

Hawaiian Legends of Old Honolulu

Hawaiian Legends of Ghosts and Ghost-Gods

Hawaiian Legends of Volcanoes

The Legends and Myths of Hawaii: The Fables and Folk-lore of a Strange People *by His Hawaiian Majesty Kalakaua*

MUSIC AND DANCE:

The Unwritten Literature of Hawaii: The Sacred Songs of the Hula *collected and translated by Nathaniel B. Emerson*

Hawaii: Music in Its History *by Ruth Hausman*

NATURAL HISTORY:

Hawaiian Herbs of Medicinal Value *by D. M. Kaaiakamanu and J. K. Akina; translated by Akaiko Akana*

Poisonous Plants of Hawaii *by Harry L. Arnold*

Manual of Wayside Plants of Hawaii *by Willis T. Pope*

Hawaiian Flowers and Flowering Trees *by Loraine E. Kuck and Richard C. Tongg*

Tropical Gardening: A Handbook for the Home Gardener *by Peggy Hickok Hodge*

Hawaiian Land Mammals *by Raymond J. Kramer*

Birds of Hawaii *by George C. Munro*

Sea Shells of the World with Values *by A. Gordon Melvin*

Seashell Parade *by A. Gordon Melvin*

Pacific Sea Shells *by Spencer Wilkie Tinker*

Sharks and Rays *by Spencer Wilkie Tinker and Charles J. DeLuca*

TRAVEL AND PICTORIAL:

The Hawaiian Guide Book for Travelers *by Henry M. Whitney*

CHARLES E. TUTTLE COMPANY

PUBLISHERS

Rutland, Vermont 05701 U. S. A.

Suido 1-chome, 2-6, Bunkyo-ku, Tokyo, Japan